IT'S TIME FOR A CHANGE

It's Time for a Change
Partnering with God for Authentic Transformation

Dr. Martin Sanders
Foreword by Dr. Leighton Ford

Edited by Eric Sanders, Nyack, NY.

Cover by Henry Kim, 180 Media Group, New York, NY.

Interior formatting by Anne McLaughlin, Blue Lake Design, Dickinson, Texas.

ISBN 978-0-9893426-0-5

Published by Global Leadership Press, Nyack, NY

First printing 2013

Printed in the United States

TABLE OF CONTENTS

ACKNOWLEDGMENTS

I owe much to a few people who have made this book possible.

To Eric Sanders, you have proven to be a magician in reworking these talks into this readable format.

To Danny Cheong, director of Global Leadership and project manager, you have taken the book from concept to reality in an unbelievably tight timeframe. Well done.

To Fred and Lynn Schumm, your dream and financial support to publish materials for Global Leadership has proven effective on several continents. Well done, good and faithful servants.

To Henry Kim and 180 Media Group, you make us look good.

To our readers, Catherine Cha Cheong and Kevin Kriesel, thanks for your insights.

To Pat Springle, thanks for your wisdom at coordinating the project.

To churches who have encountered these talks and helped to make them better, Living Christ (Nyack, NY), Subi Church (Perth, Australia), and Whitford Church (Perth, Australia).

To the Nyack College/Alliance Theological Seminary administration, thanks for partnering in this project. To the Global Leadership Associates, Dr. Chuck and Ingrid Davis, Rev. Greg and Dr. Tamie Downes, Rev. David and Ty King, Dr. Jayson and the late E.J. Park, Dr. Rob and Jennifer Reimer, Dr. Ron and Wanda Walborn, and Dr. John and Shannon Torres.

FOREWORD

Some years ago I received a letter from a seminary professor, inquiring as to whether he could take part in our Arrow Leadership Program. Since the program focused on younger leaders, I wondered why a professor would want to come. But since he was interested in leadership development we invited him as a guest.

When he walked into our opening session we saw a giant of a man, with an impressive beard and even more impressive countenance, with huge strengths that he brought – and carried lightly.

Martin, I soon learned, came with a spirit of humility, not to teach (though he could have done that) but to learn. He did not stand off as some kind of "advanced" senior leader, but was among younger men and women as a peer. At the same time it was soon evident that he had much to share, and these aspiring leaders were drawn to him as to a magnet – not only a magnetic personality but to the spirit of wisdom that was evident.

Since then Martin and I have become good friends, and he has been both a member of my own mentoring Point Group but also a teacher and mentor both through Global Leadership and in many other venues.

I am delighted that Martin has now put in print the material he has taught around the world on life change – deep and healing and transforming change, the kind in which God makes "all things new." This teaching will be a source of life change for many.

Martin himself has experienced life changing times, and often through struggle and pain – from the time of his first coming to faith when a huge hay wagon fell on him, to an accident which has left him in constant pain from a broken foot, to the challenges he has gone through with his much loved family.

One of the team members who has worked closely with Martin says that while he has learned a great deal from Martin's lectures, it has been in the daily interactions in the office that he has gained the most – seeing how he treats students, fellow professors, and strangers, with love, respect, and compassion – with consistency.

That sense of truth lived out, of life change evident in daily situations, is what you will find as you read.

And my prayer is that as Martin shares out of the deep places in his own heart, you will find the deep places in yourself touched, healed, and changed by the power of God's Spirit.

Leighton Ford, President
Leighton Ford Ministries
Charlotte, North Carolina

INTRODUCTION

Sometimes it hits you – it's time for a change. You know it. The people closest to you know it. God knows it. The need echoes deep in the chambers of your mind, heart, and soul. But how do you make that change? Where do you turn? What do you do?

Although the challenge for authentic life change would appear to be universal, the long-term success rate is rare. We love stories of dramatic change, but if you track the enduring effects, sadly, they are more often than not, lacking.

Starting something is easy. You've already started your journey towards authentic life change by choosing to read this book rather than the latest pop-fiction or watching TV. But how do you make sure this is not another false start? How do you make sure the changes you want to make not only happen, but become part of your new, true character?

There are a variety of approaches: behavior modification, wishing and hoping, psychotherapy, prayer, the list goes on and on. But when life change is necessary and/or urgent, you don't want to try a hit-and-miss approach. It needs to be clear, concise, and workable.

In this book, I hope that you will discover the unique partnership between God and your soul. We will give you an approach that is both developmental (steps and stages) and transformational (a spiritual revolution). Through this process, you will learn that change takes hard work, help from others, and the power of God. God will be willing to do His part, but as He will tell you, "It's time to do your part."

In his book, *The Two Percent Difference*, John Trent, renowned counselor and author, indicates that the expectations for authentic change need to be framed and focused. After decades of practice, he believes that most people can change approximately two percent at a time. Through the thousands of personal stories of life change that I have been part of, I concur that life change at its best will be direct, incremental and intentional. Over time, as you put together a series of these two percent changes, you will discover large-scale significant outcome.

Throughout the book, the connection between the human experience and the empowerment of God's divine presence will be considered from numerous angles. A number of the chapters will focus on understanding, updating, and expanding your soul. Your soul is the best and the worst of who you are and could be; but the soul can be reframed, redirected, and redeemed. With a renovated soul, life takes on a uniquely different feel.

So relax and settle in; you are about to experience what can happen when a willing spirit meets divine intervention. The two forces will come together in such a way that you will experience a kind of authentic life change that many people only dream about.

So let's go after this with all your heart, and see what the next section of your life can look like.

Finally, this is intentionally a short book. The real time, commitment, and work however, are in the applications at the end of each chapter. They are broken into two parts, Questions for Further Reflection, and Action Plan. I recommend spending a few days to a few weeks, answering and applying the applications thoroughly, then moving on to the next chapter.

Without the applications, this is just another book to make you feel a little better about yourself, then go on living the same old life. But as the title clearly states, this is a book about life change, and life change, as we'll see, actually takes work.

So spend an hour or so reading, and then spend the next while working through that stubborn last page at the end of each chapter. It won't be easy, it won't always be fun, but it will help you make those difficult life changes that you know it's time to make.

CHAPTER 1

IT'S TIME FOR A CHANGE

I have always been interested in life change. Why do people change? Why don't people change? What does it take to change? I am not alone. Life change is a multi-billion dollar industry.

The modern fitness craze is one aspect, and admittedly one I research more than participate in, so I know that 80% of all fitness equipment is sold between December 15th and New Year's Day. Research also shows that by Easter, 85% of that equipment will not be used again. Every shopping center has a fitness center and a "nutrition" store stock-piled with pills and powders. There's also tanning, nail and beauty salons, (though rarely a bookstore strangely enough). When you do find the rare, bookstore, there are entire self-help sections: get-rich-quick, get-thin-quick, be-better-quick.

Rehab is another relatively new phenomenon, with the 28-day stint being the most common. Yet the statistics on post-rehab relapses are sobering.

Cosmetic surgery is now big business, with over 10 million procedures being performed each year in the U.S. alone.

Then there is the lottery. In 2012, Americans spent 78 billion dollars on lotto tickets, yet you are fifty times more likely to get struck by lightning than you are to win the lottery.

As you can see, life change is hard to come by. Yet the quest endlessly continues.

I grew up in a large, loving family in rural Midwest America. My father was a successful farmer, inventor and businessman. My mother loved everyone and cooked wondrous pies. I had two older brothers and an older sister who spoiled me.

Then, when I turned 15, my sister went to college, one brother went to war in Vietnam, my other brother was killed in an automobile accident, and my father died of a sudden heart attack. My mother was swindled out of the family business and had to go to work as a waitress, and I was left to run the family farm, work on another farm, plus try to be a normal high school student.

My life had changed drastically due to external circumstances. I didn't have a say in the matter. I just worked hard and tried to adapt to my new life. But I tell you, that the dreadful external changes that befell my life as a teenager were nothing compared to the internal changes I have had to make throughout my life.

Much of our lives consist of internal circumstances, and often, we deal with them the same way I dealt with what happened to my world when I was 15. We put our heads down, keep working and accept things as they are. But it doesn't have to be like that. We can change. We can change the way we relate to ourselves, to others, and to God.

There's a catch though, it takes a lot of hard work, we need the help of others, and we need the help, love and power of God. If you have a Bible, take a look at Matthew chapter 19. If you don't have a Bible, get one.

In Matthew chapter 19, we have one of the great Jesus stories. A young rich guy comes to Jesus looking for life change. In verse 16, the guy, (known as The Rich Young Ruler) says, "Teacher, what good thing must I do if I am to inherit eternal life?"

The Rich Young Ruler came seeking Jesus, which is what people have done for a couple thousand years. All sorts of people came seeking Jesus; those who wanted hope, those who wanted help, those who needed healing, those for whom nothing short of a miracle was going to do it. Rich young rulers, hookers and lepers; they all came looking for Jesus. It really does beg the question, Why Jesus? Of all the people you could search for and seek out, from the first century until now —why Jesus? Why is Easter still a big day? It's because Jesus had, (and still has) this amazing reputation for helping people change. No matter who you are or what you've done, no matter your circumstances or need; Jesus knows and He delivers.

Christians are really good at life *after* death, but often we don't know what to say to people who are looking for real-life stuff. We say, "I don't know, but when you're ready to die, call me." But this young rich guy is saying, "Look, I want to know about the afterlife, but I need to know about life too. How should I live?"

People tend to look for everything in the wrong places. They look for happiness in money and for soul-mates in dimly lit places. People look for life change in career shifts or fitness programs. We think if we do the right things, we'll have a good life, and if we live a good life, we'll be alright in the afterlife. But for the Rich Young Ruler, and for us, life change must occur in the soul.

In Matthew 19, verse 17: Jesus said to The Rich Young Ruler, "Why do you ask me about what is good? There is only One who is good. But, if you want to enter into life, then obey the commandments."

"Which ones?"

Jesus said, "Don't kill anyone. Don't cheat on your woman. Don't steal or lie. Take care of your family and friends."

The guy said, "All these things I have kept. What am I still lacking?"

Now I don't care how good your original Greek or Aramaic is; you can't tell if the guy is a bit cynical saying, "Yeah, yeah, yeah. That's your best shot, to keep the commandments?"

You don't know if he's like an accountant, saying, "Done that, done that, done that."

We don't know if he's sincere, saying, "Okay, you're giving me some pretty good stuff, but I've done all that. What do I still lack?"

Here's what we do know; this guy was looking for very specific answers, something easy, something now. Do you know anybody else like that? I bet you have a friend like that.

Because of what I do, I get to listen to the personal stories of hundreds of people per year. Several years ago, I started interviewing people and asking them a series of three questions. I've kept track of 800 conversations now. The questions go like this:

- Since you decided to follow Jesus, what has changed most in your life?

- What hasn't changed in your life that maybe you thought would or should have?

- What's kept you from changing more?

What I have found most surprising through this short questionnaire is the redundancy of answers. There are not many different reasons people don't change. The single most common answer is, "I tried." But see, that's the problem; they keep trying to deal with their problems, over and over and over again using the same approach, which most commonly is, "try harder, do better."

If you find yourself going to God for the same failures all the time, you need to understand that because of who God is, He'll forgive you. He'll keep forgiving. But I want you to put yourself in his place for just a moment. Have you ever had a friend who continually let you down? Constantly breaks plans. Maybe they lied to you or betrayed your trust. You're still that person's friend, always will be, because that's what you are, a friend.

"Abuser of the grace of God" is not a label you want.

So you've gotta ask yourself one key question, 'Am I really ready to change?'

It's a question The Rich Young Ruler had to face. 'Am I really ready to change? Or do I simply want some relief from the shame and the guilt?'

Notice the outcome of this story: "When the young man heard what Jesus had said, he asked, 'What do I still lack?'"

Jesus said, "If you want to be made perfect, go and sell your possessions and give them to the poor. Then you'll have treasure in heaven and then come and follow Me."

When the young man heard this, he walked away sad, because of his great wealth. Notice that Jesus let him walk away.

Now at this point, I always say, "I don't like this story anymore." I like the fun Jesus stories. The ones where everybody gets healed and the devil gets his butt kicked. I love it when people with no hope get hope. I love it when people need a miracle, and they get it. But this guy decides to walk away, and Jesus lets him. You know the guy had a bunch of money. He could have built Jesus a brand new church building. I'd have said, "Let's work out a deal. Let's do 20% this year, with an annual readjustment.

Who knows, after a few years when you have enough equity in, we can do a reverse tithe plan. Let's negotiate."

But Jesus knew that money wasn't the issue, nor was it behavior. The Rich Young Ruler had everything under control. He needed to *relinquish* control.

The key is to ask yourself, "What are the control issues that keep me from following Jesus fully?"

The Rich Young Ruler came looking for one thing, a deep satisfaction that his perfect life and perfect behavior couldn't offer, and all he had to do was walk away from it all, and go traveling around with the man himself.

I travel too much, partly because I love it. If Jesus told me, "Martin, you need to quit your job and hit the road with me," I wouldn't even put in my two weeks' notice.

Unfortunately, God does not think that's what I need. I have my own set of issues. We all do.

Because I was a pastor, our family vacations always started on Sunday afternoons. This Sunday was Easter, and after church, we were driving from Chicago to Florida. We were doing the great American family thing: four kids, van, camper, Disney World, the whole bit.

On Saturday, I was spiritually getting ready to preach for Easter, but I was also physically getting ready to spend a week and 1,500 hundred miles in a van with my family. Dianna, my wife, said, "Before we leave, you've gotta get new shoes."

"I'm wearing my cowboy boots."

She said, "Not on the beach you're not."

"But we're traveling. You gotta wear cowboy boots if you're traveling."

"The shoe store in the mall's having a big sale. Go!"

"It's Saturday. Men do not go to the mall on Saturday. If they do, they rarely come back alive."

"Quit your whining and go get the shoes. You need them!"

I drove to the mall. I was a pastor, and it was Easter weekend. I was all prayed up, so I got a good spot by the entrance three doors down from the shoe store.

I was the only guy in the store. I found the pair I was looking for and the salesman asked, "Can I help you?"

"I hope so. I need these shoes, size 13, incredibly wide. Do you have them?"

"I doubt it."

"Please check."

He comes back and says, "This is your lucky day. I have 'em. They're on sale."

I'm thinking, 'It's the day before Easter. I'm a pastor. This is my time. I tried 'em on, they fit, they're on sale. The whole trip's going to take less than an hour. It's a miracle.'

But as I start to pay for them, he says, "Can I get you anything else?"

"Nope, this is all I need."

He looked down and he said, "Looks to me like you need a new pair of boots."

"I'm sure I do, but not today. I just want to pay for these shoes, please."

"Fine. But, honestly, you do need a new pair of boots."

"I'm very aware I need boots, but I'm going to Florida and my wife would prefer if I wore shoes instead of boots. You have the shoes I want, they're on sale, they fit me. Please, let me pay for them."

"Okay, but I have a responsibility as a shoe salesman to tell you, you need a new pair of boots."

I took a deep sigh.

"Tell you what," the guy says. "I'll make you a deal."

"I already have a deal."

"Let me make you a better deal. You pay full price for the sneakers; I'll throw in a new pair of boots –free."

"Why would you do that?"

"You just seem like a good guy."

"Well, you're very discerning, but why would you do it?"

"I don't know, I just want to do it for you."

"Fine."

So I pick out a new pair of boots, and as I go to pay for them, he says, "Here's the deal. You have to pay full price for the sneakers, I'll throw in the new pair of boots free, but, you have to leave your old boots here."

I just stared at the guy, and he says, "You're a preacher, aren't you?"

"How do you know that?"

"I've seen you around."

"What, you like really big men?"

"My kids go to school with your kids. We live around the corner from you. Tomorrow's Easter isn't it?"

"It is."

"I've not been to church in 25 years. Would it be okay if we come?"

He came to church the following day and I ended my sermon with the boot story. I said, "It is a perfect picture of the offer God gives you. Brand new pair of whatever you need, free. Just one catch, you gotta be willing to leave the old ones behind."

On the way out of church, he grabbed me and gave me a giant bear-hug.

It's the miracle of a new life in Christ, but you've got to be willing to leave the old stuff behind. It's time for a change.

QUESTIONS FOR FURTHER REFLECTION

1. In what ways have I actively sought after Jesus in the past few months?

2. What is the one thing that will hold me back from life change?

3. In my life change process, what might be the next step?

ACTION PLAN

1. Fast and pray for at least 24 hours, preferably two or three days.

CHAPTER 2

TIME TO DEAL WITH YOUR DARK SIDE

I am the president and founder of a non-profit organization called Global Leadership, which focuses on developing and mentoring the next generation of leaders.

I started 'Global' in my late thirties. As the 'developmental stage' of my life drew to a close, I began looking at the needs of the world and the church, and found a gaping hole; Christian leaders are largely trained in the classroom, by non-leader academics, and then are sent into the field with little to no continued intentional development.

In attempting to develop top-level leaders, one thing we establish very early is called, 'the discipline of honesty'.

We hold up a metaphorical mirror, and talk about what the authentic life looks like. Then we identify ways that we deceive ourselves, and enter into a covenant with ourselves, other people, and God, to develop a discipline of honesty.

It's fascinating how many highly effective people find this extremely challenging. It's so much easier to blame others, excuse yourself and put a subtle spin on reality. The pattern doesn't get better with time; therefore it is time to enter the no-excuse zone.

Psalm 51 is one of the noted Psalms of David. After David's very public failures and humiliations, he asks the Father of his soul, "Can I reconnect with You?" David pleads with God, even argues, saying, "We had a covenant." God is the great covenant maker of the universe, and we humans are the great covenant breakers.

The Psalmist says, "We had a deal. I've let my end down. You have not. Can we please go back and reestablish our promises to each other?"

The Hebraic definition of "covenant" is an agreement between a stronger party and a weaker party. It should be obvious, but when you enter into a covenant with God, you are always the weaker party. In this covenant, God is literally offering Himself. Please don't miss this; the great God of the universe, the Creator of all that exists, the Father of your soul, offers Himself to you.

The Psalmist then goes on to ask if God will, "Help him deal with his iniquities." The word 'iniquity' means to take something good and honest, and twist it, ever so subtly, so that it becomes unhealthy and improper.

David is saying, "God, I'm a passionate man. I'm passionate about You. I'm passionate about being the leader of Your people. I'm passionate as a warrior and a leader of the armies.

I'm passionate about my family. I'm passionate about my wives, all of them." Therein lies part of the problem.

David's passion was good and healthy, but it got shifted ever so subtly, until it became something that led him astray. Very, very far astray. Like, having a man murdered because you impregnated his wife astray.

King David slept with Bathsheba while her husband was off fighting a war for his king – King David to be exact. Pretty bad, right? David didn't think so. 'People make mistakes. No one has to know. Oh, wait, she's pregnant? Still, we'll just grant Uriah leave so he can come home and sleep with his wife, and raise my kid as his own.'

A decent plan, but David forgot that many other people held on to their sense of loyalty, duty and honesty. Uriah had taken a soldier's oath, which among other things, required him to stay celibate while on active duty. Instead of sleeping with his wife, Uriah slept on the stone floor of the barracks with the other men. David was growing desperate, so he pulled some kingly strings and had Uriah sent to the frontlines, ensuring that he died in battle.

In other Psalms, Psalm 26 for instance, David says, with bellowing passion, "Vindicate me, O God, for I have walked in my integrity."

Whenever I read this, I laugh and say, "David we should probably have a talk. I'm not sure you should be the national spokesperson for integrity. David, let's play a game. Did you ever watch *Sesame Street*? Remember the song, 'One of these things is not like the others / One of these things just doesn't belong?' David, Uriah, Bathsheba, Integrity. Which one doesn't belong?"

But you see, David understood something that we either never learned or have forgotten. To be a person of integrity doesn't mean you do not mess up. To be a person of integrity means that you deal honestly with all of your failures, vices and bad habits.

Psalm 51 is split in the middle. The tone in verses 1-9 is different than from verse ten onwards. In the second half of the Psalm, we see a humbler David. Verses 10-12 are well known within the broader community of faith. We have spun them in countless songs. In the original Hebraic form, these are six one-line requests. Notice, they can all stand alone. Each one is a clear and concise request of God:

- Create in me a clean heart

- Renew a right spirit within me

- Do not cast me away from your presence

- Do not take your Holy Spirit from me

- Restore to me the joy of your salvation

- Sustain me with a willing spirit.

What David is saying is, "God, because I know myself and my very real ability to mess up, even with the best of intentions, will Your Holy Spirit partner with my human spirit so that we can do this together? Because I've not done well on my own, I'm asking for Your help. It's the only way it will work. Help me. Help me, please."

David was aware that he couldn't try harder, be better, do more. He had failed miserably trying to do it by his own strength. He needed help, which should have been obvious. I mean, when you're sleeping with a married woman and then having her husband murdered, it's probably time you get some help, and not just coffee with a friend.

Now, David was a public figure. His mistakes affected many people and his attempts to cover them up involved many people. Most of us though, live mostly private lives, so our issues are not nearly as public. Consequently, we think we can hide from our issues, and hide the implications of these issues from those closest to us. Some of us even hide our dark sides from ourselves. I have actually had people say to me, "I'm not sure I have a dark side."

To them, I always suggest that they ask the three people who know them best, "If I have a dark side, what might it be?" Many people have reported back to me with great shock and sadness, that all three people mentioned the exact same issue.

Even if you are blind to your own dark issues, those who know you and love you most are keenly aware of them and are hoping and praying that you will take on the discipline of honesty and actively bring those dark areas of your life to the light and deal with them.

Other people know they have a dark side; they just don't deal with it, either because it's too hard, or they're embarrassed, or they think that no one's getting hurt, or that no one will find out.

Jack had a privileged upbringing. His father was a successful international businessman, and he sent his son to an elite sporting school where he became a victim of sexual abuse. Jack was now in his late forties, married with a child, but he struggled with tendencies of sexual attraction towards children.

Jack was in a group of men who wanted to be honest about their life and struggles, and he decided he could trust this group with his.

Jack had to go on a business trip, but he made an agreement with his accountability partner from the group to call as soon as he landed. Jack didn't. His accountability partner called him repeatedly. Jack eventually picked up the phone, and admitted that he was sitting in his rental car outside of a playground.

His partner said, "I'm proud of you for answering the phone and admitting that. Now drive back to the airport, take the first flight home, and we'll get you some help."

No matter what your issue is, no matter how dark, or socially unacceptable, there is hope, and help, but not without honesty.

By design, humans are intended to be in relationship, both with tight-knit groups, and broader communities. As such, the unresolved issues of our own heart and soul impact and influence others around us, far more than most of us consider.

I hope that you have at some point in your life played Pac Man. In the video game, Pac Man (Pac Woman) goes all over the screen devouring bite-sized pellets. If you do not deal with your dark side, it will take on the role of a Pac Man, eating straight through your soul. Then it'll turn around and come back and keep repeating the process until all that is left is a hollow shell and a finely polished image.

It's time to go after the dark side. Do it for God's sake. Do it for your own sake. Do it for the sake of those who love you most. Do it for the sake of the community and the people who have to interact with you.

But how?

The first thing is to enter the No Excuse Zone. No blaming, no whining, no excuses. It is time to own your life – all of it.

One of the most effective ways to do this is what has been called a guided prayer. This is where you block off two hours and invite the Spirit of God to come and lead you back through your life to identify anything that needs to be addressed. It helps to work through this is in age categories: birth to the age of five, six to twelve years old, the teen years, the college years, the young adult years, and then from young adulthood until today.

Through Global Leadership, we have used this same model to address the compulsive patterns in the lives of hundreds of people in dozens of cultural contexts, to help them take personal responsibility, and to deal with their own dark sides.

The first time I went through a guided prayer was in my late 30's. I had been struggling with some addictive and compulsive tendencies (primarily sexual), that I was having a hard time controlling. I had tried all the classic models: therapy and counseling, talking and praying with a mentor, sheer willpower but nothing seemed to break the pattern; very little seemed to even help. I decided to ask a personal friend and a trusted, older man of wisdom if I could have an afternoon of their time, where they would listen to a confession of my life. This is not something I looked forward to, but I knew that I needed to do it if I was going to break the pattern and move on with my life.

We met and got underway with very little structure. I simply began pulling up memories and talking them through, while they listened and discerned. Sometimes our eyes were open, sometimes they were closed. The afternoon progressed with very little fanfare.

At one stage, I was disclosing some humiliating things. I remember looking across the room at my friend and asking, "Am I okay?"

He just gave a quiet nod, encouraging me to keep going.

It took two and a half hours for me to go through everything, and when I finished, the older man of wisdom said, "I just want to do a couple of more things." As a missionary among tribal peoples of Indonesia, he knew it was important to make sure some, "spiritual and curse things" were broken.

Through this process, I discovered that my addictive and compulsive tendencies were much more expansive than I had originally thought. I wish I could tell you that the day ended with some dramatic flair. It did not. It ended very quietly. I went home, not quite sure what to even think or feel, but the compulsions that I had not been able to handle, broke that day and have not returned since.

Sometimes though, more extreme actions are required.

After I finished speaking at a couple's seminar in Detroit, a young, good looking couple came to me and said they wanted to talk, "privately."

It turned out she had extreme anger issues. She would regularly hit and punch her husband.

I asked, "How serious are you about fixing this problem?"

She said, "I love him, more than anything in the world. I can't lose him, but, I just can't control myself."

I told her, "Then if you ever hit him again, get a knife, and cut the tip of your little finger off."

The next time I was in Detroit, the couple once again came up to me after I had finished speaking, this time accompanied by her parents. The woman held up her hand, now with the tip of her little finger missing.

The parents said, "Thank you for helping our daughter. She was so bad for so long. We thought she'd end up either dead or in prison. Now she's just missing a nail."

Now if this sounds extreme, switch the genders in this story, and imagine a man that can't quit beating his wife.

It's time. It's time for a change. It's time to honestly and directly address your dark side. You might not have to cut off the tip of your little finger, but it's going to take hard work, sacrifice and you're going to need help.

QUESTIONS FOR FURTHER REFLECTION

1. What are the "self-talk" phrases that I use that are really excuses or blaming someone else?

2. What restitution, apology, or sacrifice, beyond repentance and confessing, do I have to make?

ACTION PLAN

1. I will own my "junk" personally and before God, and actively enter a "no excuse, no blaming, no whining zone."

2. I will actively pursue areas of restitution and restoring situations and relationships where I have been less than forthcoming.

CHAPTER 3

IT'S TIME TO MAKE
PEACE WITH YOUR PAST

It's intriguing to me that most of psychology has been co-opted by people, not only outside the church, but often outside of the realms of the Christian faith.

If we were to survey a hundred people on any city street, and ask the question, "If you were to have a significant psychological need, where would you go for help?" Very few people would respond, "The church."

When churches first started inviting Alcoholics Anonymous and other related groups to hold meetings in their church, they realized the profound impact it was having on their community. One major component to any step-oriented program is making peace with your past, and churches became keenly aware that a healed soul is a vital step on the path to life change.

A few years ago, I was speaking at a conference in East Germany, which was hosting young leaders from eleven countries. As a part of the conference, we did a seminar on emotional development and simply stated that, if the participants wanted to expand their emotional frameworks experientially, we would do a public manhood/womanhood ceremony. Part of this ceremony would be to leave behind the things that they felt were limiting them, and call them into the fullness of their identity, the fullness of their manhood/womanhood, and the fullness of their future and destiny in God.

Many of the conference's participants immediately came to us and said, "This is uncomfortable and awkward for us; we don't want to do this."

I said, "That's fine, it's not a requirement. We only said that if there are enough people who wanted this, we'd do it."

We met in an old stone chapel that had been bombed during World War II. One by one, we listened to young leaders stand and express what they wanted to leave behind and then what they wanted to ask the Father of their soul to give them.

We then created a human corridor with a line of people on each side. As each participant walked through the corridor, each person on the line would reach out a hand and touch them, some would say a word or two; some would simply give a gentle touch. When they arrived at the front the leaders would pray for and bless them.

The ceremony stretched into the early morning hours as participant after participant were freed from the things that had entrapped them and they asked that the Father of their soul to give them the best of His gifts as they moved ahead.

In Psalm 103, a picture emerges of God as the Father who heals your soul, so you can be free and full with an expanded capacity to love and be loved.

The first five verses of Psalm 103 read: "Bless the LORD, O my soul; and all my innermost being, praise his holy name. Bless the LORD, O my soul, and forget not all his benefits: who forgives all of your sins, heals all of your diseases, who redeems your life from the pit and crowns you with love and compassion."

There are some seven words for 'soul' used in the Bible; but the one used in this Psalm appears to be unique. The word for soul here is literally, "throat." If it was translated literally, it would read, "Bless the LORD, O my throat." Not exactly a catchy worship song. But you see the ancients understood that all of life passes through our throats: air, water, food. The throat is so vital that two fingers strategically placed can terminate one's life. Thus, the Psalmist is saying, "I want to get where I can thank, praise and bless the Lord with all that I am, as a complete, whole person."

The twelve-step programs have long known something that we have not. To experience real, sustainable life change to the point where you become a whole person that can love God and others with your entire being, you must make peace with your past. This is not just about getting rid of the old thoughts, feelings, and behaviors. It is about embracing the best of what the Father of your soul has for you.

A year ago, a female friend called me with great excitement in her voice and inquired, "Martin, did you watch Oprah today?"

I responded, "I didn't happen to catch that one."

"That's what I thought," she said. "So I have ordered a copy of today's program to be sent to you overnight. Will you please watch it within the next week and get back to me?"

The next day, to honor my commitment to my friend, I sat down with a bowl of popcorn to watch Oprah. As the one-hour program unfolded, Oprah had seven women tell their stories of being terribly hurt, abused, neglected, and abandoned. Oprah matter-of-factly told each one, "You know you have to forgive."

Every one of the panelists resisted, saying, "But you don't understand how badly they hurt me."

Oprah responded, "You're right. I don't understand your particular story, but I know my own story. I also know that if you don't forgive that person, then that incident will always have control over you. It will always have a hold on your life. If you don't forgive, you will never be free."

As I sat there, somewhat stunned, I thought, 'You go, Oprah. You get this. You may get this better than the church.'

Oprah understands what God demonstrated through his Son; that forgiveness, even if it wasn't asked for, is a vital component to healing.

Psalm 103 says, "As high as the heavens are above the earth, so great is the love of the Father of your soul for you. As far as the east is from the west, so far has He removed our transgressions from us."

Picture yourself climbing a mountain. Take your time – the air gets thinner as you ascend. When you reach the summit, absorb the grandeur of the view. Look to the east, the rising of the sun. Enjoy the beauty and wonder of it all. Now turn and look to the west, as far as you can. Contemplate the distance from horizon to horizon.

Now, take your time descending the mountain. Meander down until you come to an expansive body of water, whether a great lake or an ocean. Feel the breeze and hear the waves. Gaze across the surface as far as you can.

"As far as the east is from the west, so far has He removed our transgressions from us."

Micah 7:19 reads: "God will have compassion on us, will tread our sins underfoot and bury them into the depths of the sea."

Your sins and the bad things you've experienced are gone. You are released. The Father of your soul releases you to make peace with your past.

I had led a weekend leadership conference in western Canada for a group of eight churches. We finished Saturday evening, and I was to speak at one of the churches the following morning. I had enjoyed being with the people from that church, but they seemed to have difficulty experiencing the forgiveness of God.

On Sunday afternoon, I asked the senior pastor if, in the evening service, I could do something very specific about forgiveness. I expressed my observation that they were great people, but it felt like they were living under a cloud of shame and guilt. Many of them seemed to do very good things, but possibly for some wrong reasons. The pastor said that he trusted me. I told him, "I want to structure a simple service: twenty minutes of worship, a twenty-minute sermon, and we'll leave twenty minutes for a response. If no one responds, the two of us will take off and grab some pizza."

The service went as planned. A great twenty-minute worship set, I finished the sermon in nineteen and a half minutes, and simply let the congregation know that if they wanted to feel forgiven tonight, there would be people at the front who could pray with them, or they could just have some quiet moments alone.

I said, "There will be no classic invitation, no additional request, no emotional push or pull. This is your time to connect with the Father of your soul."

As the worship team struck the first chords, the center aisle filled with people who apparently wanted to be prayed for. It was overwhelming as I stood at the front with the senior pastor.

I immediately turned to him and said, "I thought we had elders and prayer teams with us. Where are they?"

He said, "Front of the line."

It became quite clear that receiving prayer was going to take some time, so people began to bypass the line and kneel in the front or beside the pews. Some lay on the floor or propped themselves up in a corner. They started sniffling, then crying.

The pastor turned to me and said, "I am very uncomfortable with this."

I said, "Me too. Do you want to shut it down?"

"No. We got it started. We've got to finish this thing. Keep praying."

It soon grew very loud in that auditorium. The sniffling had turned to weeping and a few had actually turned it into wailing. Wailing makes everyone uncomfortable. You want to rescue and help, but if someone's at the point of wailing, they just need to get it out. It took some two hours and twenty minutes to pray for everyone who wanted prayer that night.

As soon as we finished, the pastor turned to me and said, "I want to see you in my study."

When we sat in his study, he leaned back in his chair and asked, "What happened out there?"

I responded, "I think I may have been right, your congregation needed to feel God's forgiveness."

After a brief silence he stated, "I've done this to them, haven't I."

"Oh, it goes well beyond you," I assured him. "It's the families they've come from, schools, organizations, community psyche, and previous churches. What happens is, in wanting to do well, we put extra pressure on people. They want to do good things that seem to matter in the bigger picture, but in doing so, we heap shame and guilt on them."

"I think I need to be prayed for as well." And as if on cue, there was a knock on the door. It was one of the elders asking, "Do you guys need anything?"

I said, "Why don't you go get the pastor's wife and another elder and come and join us for a bit more prayer?" That night, we also prayed the pastor through a release of his own soul.

It was fun to see what happened in that church. In a matter of five months, attendance grew by 30%. Peoples' lives really did seem to change. It was the same people, same preaching, same worship team, but the people were different. They were free. They'd been released, and a fullness had come into their soul.

This is what God desires for you; to be free of your past so that you can love Him with all of your throat.

QUESTIONS FOR FURTHER REFLECTION

1. Can I identify any leftover issues from the past or things hidden in my soul that need to be exposed and brought into the light?

2. How long has it been since I've done some form of absolute confession, both to God and to a trusted friend? Is it time for another round?

3. Is there any lie or subtle deception I tell myself to soothe my conscience?

ACTION PLAN

1. Become a person who tells the complete truth rather than a portion of the truth.

2. Look at my relationships and family connections to see if there are any secrets or lies that need to be exposed or brought into the light.

CHAPTER 4

IT'S TIME TO GO AFTER YOUR GREATEST LIMITATIONS

When I was a professor and counselor in Canada, I had a handful of pastors coming to see me, all with intense anger issues. Canada has a great social service system, so I checked to see if there were any anger resolution groups, specifically for people whose profession or personal situation made it difficult to speak of such things openly.

Immediately a new group was formed, with ten men, eight of which were pastors. Before long, there were two such groups consisting exclusively of angry ministers.

Anger is a normal, sometimes even healthy emotion, but an angry minister is generally not a good minister, so for these men, their anger was a great limitation, both to themselves and to those around them.

Angry minister help groups don't make for glamorous stories, but it's real and perhaps more closely akin to what many of you deal with, day in and day out.

For a more dramatic example of a great limitation, let's look at Mark 9, which starting in verse 14 reads: "When Jesus came to the disciples, he saw a large crowd around them, and the teachers of the law were arguing with them. As soon as all the people saw Jesus, they were overwhelmed with wonder and they ran to greet him."

"What are you arguing with them about?" Jesus asked.

A man in the crowd answered, "Teacher, I brought my son, who is possessed by a spirit that has robbed him of speech. Whenever it seizes him, it throws him to the ground; he foams at the mouth, gnashes his teeth, and becomes rigid. I asked your disciples to drive out the spirit, but they couldn't."

"Oh unbelieving generation," Jesus replied, "… How long shall I put up with you?"

Now, you never want Jesus to say to you, 'How long shall I put up with you?'

Then Jesus said, "Bring me the boy."

When the spirit saw Jesus, it acted like it had the boys' whole life and immediately threw the boy into convulsions. He fell to the ground, rolled around, foaming at the mouth.

Whether you're a therapist, a physician, a police officer or a minister, whenever somebody comes for help, they always have what is called, "the presenting problem." The presenting problem here was dramatic. We have a boy who had what was probably epilepsy. The condition had made him mute and deaf and probably cognitively impaired as well. His condition was killing him, not simply lowering his quality of life. This is a very real presenting problem.

Over the last twenty years, I've done a number of family-life conferences in various places. It is amazing how many families come to me with what they think are significant problems with one of their children. As I listen to them, I think, 'That's not a big problem. Read Mark 9. Now *that's* a family with problems.'

This was a significant presenting problem, but I love Jesus as much for what He didn't do, as for what He did do. He didn't panic; He didn't say, "I've never seen this one before. You're really bad." He was very kind and calm in a dreadful situation, even taking time to teach his disciples. He also takes time with the family, asking, "How long has he been like this?"

"From childhood, since he was a lad. It's often thrown him into the fire or into the water trying to kill him, but if you can do anything, take pity on us and help us."

This father's in an absolutely helpless and hopeless situation. He has no idea what to do. He's got one shot. His only prayer in this whole world is to go to Jesus. He comes begging for help, and then has the audacity to say to Jesus, "If you can do anything."

I can imagine Jesus saying, "If I, if *I* can do anything? Do you know who you're talking to here?"

I wish we had first century YouTube, to see Jesus' response, like a great Robert De Niro scene, "You talkin' to me? You talkin' to me?"

When identifying the presenting problems, trained specialists also identify any possible limitations, and trust me, all of us have limitations. What we have to figure out is, are these real, did we impose them, or are they just phantoms?

Here are several limitations in this story:

The disciples lacked effectiveness. They thought they knew what to do. They didn't access the power of God; they just went through the motions, imitating what they had seen Jesus do.

The father did not have authentic faith. He just didn't know where else to go. He was desperate, but not convinced. Later this father says, "Help my unbelief."

Jesus has an incredible response to this: "Everything is possible to the one who believes."

Highlight it, write it down, create a mnemonic device so you'll never forget, but at all costs remember this: Everything is possible to the one who believes.

In academics, the term hermeneutics refers to the study of interpretation. In biblical hermeneutics, we not only look at what the text says, but also at what it doesn't say.

In this passage, Jesus is not saying, that if you just ask him, over and over and over again, you'll get everything you want. Jesus is saying, that with authentic faith, everything is possible. The father's immediate response is, "I do believe, now help me overcome my unbelief."

Having unbelief is natural. The father in this story had unbelief. Saint Doubting Thomas had unbelief. But here's the thing; Thomas doubted that Jesus had risen from the dead. That's a pretty natural thing to doubt after having just watched him die. This father had unbelief, but he had just met Jesus.

The problem is that some of us have been at this faith thing for 5, 10 or 20 years, and we are still stuck at this very elementary level of belief. The father was brand new to this faith in Jesus' thing, so he asked for a little help with his unbelief, but for many of us, it's time to step up and forget this old phrase, and instead say, "God, I believe. Now please take me to the next level. I want authentic faith. Help me."

Verse 25 says: "When Jesus saw that the crowd was running away, He rebuked this unclean spirit, saying, 'You deaf and dumb spirit, I command you, come out of him and never enter him again.'"

The spirit shrieked, convulsed the boy violently, and came out. The boy looked so much like a corpse that many of the people said, "I think he's dead." But Jesus took the boy by the hand and lifted him to his feet.

The moral of the story? No matter who you are, no matter what you have done, no matter what has happened to you, no matter what you need, Jesus knows, Jesus understands, and Jesus delivers. That's the amazing power of God that comes through His son, Jesus.

Let's talk about what it means when He delivers. As we said, this boy and his father were in a seemingly impossible situation with very real limitations: incompetent disciples, a sick boy, an unbelieving father, religious teachers naysaying in the background, a boisterous crowd that wasn't helping anything. But notice that when the crowd started running, Jesus took control of the situation quickly. His job was not to create a show or embarrass anybody; His job was to protect human dignity. He doesn't want you or your story or your issues to be exposed; He just wants you to be free of them.

Early one Christmas morning the phone rang, so I answered, "Merry Christmas." But it was not a merry Christmas on the other end of the line, where a guy said, "Martin, I know it's Christmas. I'm so sorry I'm calling you but we have a situation. My sister has had a number of tough issues in her life and for some reason they've all come to a head this morning. She's gone crazy!"

"Explain."

"I don't even know what to say. She's uncontrollable. I can't even describe all that's going on. She's locked herself in a room and we're afraid that she's either going to hurt herself or one of us. Can I send her to you?"

There was a long silence before I replied, "She's *your* sister. Why do you want to send her to me?"

"We don't know what else to do."

The next morning they put her on a plane and sent her to New York. Now I had just had major ankle surgery and the doctors had me on really good pain killers. It was Christmas and I was on drugs. My office was shut for the holidays. I really wasn't in a place to deal with this.

Here was her story: When she was 15 years old, she and a girlfriend were shopping in a mall in southern California when they were abducted by a Mexican drug gang, taken out to the desert, gang-raped and left naked on the side of the road. The other girl died. This girl crawled back out to the road where someone found her. It took the family 36 hours to locate her because there was no identification on her and she was unable to communicate coherently.

Now, almost 10 years later, she had dreadful emotional and spiritual issues. Flashbacks, nightmares, you name it. It's a tough story, but not an impossible one.

I took some pain killers and knew I had about two hours before I either passed out or the incredible pain returned, so I told her, "We'll get underway. We've got about a two hour window. I'm convinced God can do it."

We got started and made a number of simple commands into the spiritual realms. As soon as we began, she lapsed into an altered state. I wish I had received permission to have a video camera running, because you could literally watch these spirits come and take her over and she would thrash back-and-forth. You could see her fighting and making noises. She would escalate into a crescendo and go, "Ugh" before coming back down.

What was interesting for me is that in an hour and thirty-five minutes, I only said about fifteen words. It was simply the power of God at work. At the end, she blinked her eyes, and said, "I went somewhere, didn't I?"

"You did."

"And some stuff left me, didn't it?"

"It did."

"How many?"

"How many do you think?"

"It felt like seven spirits."

"I counted seven."

She immediately burst into tears. I took a few minutes to wrap up, prayed over her and put her on a plane back to California. Over the next few days I got numerous phone calls from people that I'd never met, saying, "We don't know what you did, we don't want to know, but we want you to know what an amazingly different person we have in our family now."

Notice how Mark 9 wraps up in verses 28 and 29: "After Jesus had gone indoors, his disciples asked him privately, 'Why couldn't we drive this one out?'"

Jesus replied, "This kind can come out only by prayer."

Now in some of your Bibles, there will be a parenthetical note that reads, "Some manuscripts will say, 'by prayer and fasting.'" If you research this, you'll discover that when people were reading and transcribing this passage, it just didn't make sense to them. It is as if the disciples said, "Jesus, can you be a little more thorough here? We know about the prayer thing, but what else?"

Some well-intentioned biblical scholar said, "Well, He probably meant fasting too."

Nope, just prayer.

So why didn't it work for the disciples? Why doesn't it always work for us? The disciples had seen Jesus do it, and they'd done it themselves.

In one of these impossible situations, the disciples did what we often do; we simply go with what we know. We go with our own strength. We go with what we think will work. We say, "I got this. I've seen this done. If you just do this and this, it'll happen."

But the disciples, like us, often forget about authentic faith.

We tend to toss around the word "faith." We use the word without engaging it deeply. Faith is really a kind of active trust that engages well beyond the human experience. Authentic faith is not passive. You can't take it for granted. You can't rely on your past experiences. In order to have authentic faith, you need to be engaged.

When you see two people in love, you just know it. They are totally focused on each other. Nothing else matters. It's just the two of them. Eye to eye, heart to heart, soul to soul; they're engaged. It's an emotional thing, it's a spiritual thing, it's a physiological thing, it's a physical thing; they are absolutely engaged.

That kind of engagement is what authentic faith is all about.

In 1980, I read a report in The New York Times on the Special Olympics. The reporter was at the men's 400-meter final, and he wrote, "As I sat in the stands, I looked at the two competitors, one with Cerebral palsy, the other with Down syndrome, and I thanked God that I wasn't like them."

It was late in the day and the sparse crowd was lethargic. When the loud speaker blared: runners to your mark, get set, go; the crowd showed little interest, but the coach of the athlete with Down syndrome was screaming, "Come on Joey! This is your race! You're a winner! Beat this kid!"

The reporter wrote, "It felt like the race would go on forever." To make matters worse, by the first bend Joey had a twenty-meter lead. It was going to be a long, slow, painful defeat, yet the coach never ceased his passionate chant of, "Come on Joey! You got this! Beat this kid! You're a winner!"

When Joey rounded the last bend, he was leading by fifty-meters and the once quiet crowd had drowned out the coach by chanting "Joey! Joey! Joey!" Yet twenty-meters from the finish line, this young man with Down syndrome stopped, dead in his tracks. The crowd was silenced and only Joey's coach could be heard yelling, "Come on Joey! What are you doing? You're a winner! Finish this kid!"

But Joey only turned, and, first to the coach, then to the crowd, smiled and waved. Joey looked back to his struggling competition, reached out his hand, and waited for him. The crowd erupted into uproarious celebration. As they crossed the finish line together, hand in hand, you could hear Joey's coach yelling above the crowd's cheers, "Atta boy, Joey! You're a real winner!"

What if, you're greatest limitation is not a debilitating disease? And what if your greatest attribute is not intelligence or a cool job like a New York Times reporter? What if your greatest attribute is love, kindness or the ability to empower others? What if your greatest limitation, is arrogance or a judgmental spirit?

You see, the boy in Mark 9, had a great limitation, a disease or demons that sought to destroy him. But for most of us, our greatest limitations might be something much more subtle.

There are no limits to what God can do. The only limitations are the ones we possess. It's time to identify your greatest limitations. It's time to actively engage them. It's time for a change.

QUESTIONS FOR FURTHER REFLECTION

1. Can I begin to identify and make a list of any perceived or real limitations that hinder my life change process?

2. Can I identify any ways in which I or the enemy of my soul creates patterns where I play the role of the victim?

ACTION PLAN

1. Seek out a trusted friend, prayer partner, life coach, counselor, or spiritual director to bring those limitations, "into the light."

CHAPTER 5

IT'S TIME TO INVEST
YOUR LIFE

In the parable of the talents, Jesus draws the analogy of a ruler who is going away for a time, and entrusts three different people with different amounts of money to be invested in his absence.

The moral of the story is that different people are given different things, but everyone is expected to invest what they have been given. This principle is simple and straight-forward, yet it eludes many people. Either because they're not quite sure what they have been given or they're not quite sure what to do with it.

The first part of investing your life is to be aware of what you've been given. The old saying, 'count your blessings', is often easier said than done, but it is vital to investing your life in a meaningful way. Family, health, friends, employment, and the wonder of creation. These are all things you must be consciously aware of if you are going to invest in them, and utilize them to invest in others.

The second key is to become comfortable with yourself and to be aware of your inherent strengths and weaknesses.

Whenever I speak on this topic, people always come up to me and say, "I'm not certain of my abilities and giftings." There's usually one person who says, "I'm not sure I have any."

My approach is to be very direct. My simple response is, "I don't know you very well, but if you give me three minutes, I'm quite confident I can give you your top three unique abilities."

This is easy for me to do in other people, because usually, the issue is not a lack of ability, but the inability to utilize them. Additionally, we don't get to choose our giftings, and often, we wish we had different abilities than we really do.

In leadership development, we use a variety of assessments: personal, developmental, emotional, and spiritual. One such assessment tool is called, 'IDAK' (*Discovering Your Natural Talents* by John Bradley). The IDAK assessment does not rate your strengths and weaknesses; it only identifies your greatest strength. IDAK begins by asking for the 10 best experiences of your life, and then offers suggestions as to what you should do. When I took my IDAK assessment, it offered me four suggestions:

1) I should be a speaker or trainer.

2) I should become a university president.

3) I should create my own developmental organization.

4) I should market agricultural products. (If this one doesn't seem to fit, you should know that to the best of my knowledge, I am the only Professor of Theology and certified artificial cattle inseminator in the country, maybe the world.)

I have accomplished most of the things the IDAK suggested I'd be good at. But what the test does not tell you is how much work goes into achieving these goals. What this test doesn't show are the 14 years I spent earning multiple degrees, all while working full-time and raising four children with my wonderful wife. What it doesn't show are those early mornings in the early years of our family, when Dianna and I would put sleeping children in our old beat up car and deliver papers before she went to wait tables and I went to class to study ancient Hebrew.

Life progress and change takes hard work, but many people are willing to put in the effort; they just don't know *how* to do it.

Early in my career, I came to the conclusion that most leaders, ministers or therapists, have never actually shown people how to invest their lives. Even the people, who led *successful* lives, were not always good at *investing* their lives.

I've always felt I had a good life. I never made much money, but I have a great family, I get to travel lots and see people's lives changed.

One of the perks to flying a hundred thousand miles a year is upgrading to first class. It's always interesting to talk to the business executives who sit beyond the great dividing curtain.

The conversations usually start in a pretty standard way:

"Business or pleasure?" "On your way to or from home?" "What do you do?"

If I'm feeling talkative, I say, "I lecture on developing leaders and investing your life in the kingdom of God."

Often, I only get blank stares in return, but sometimes I will hear, "I'd give anything to do what you do, because what you do matters. Although I make a great living at what I do, it does not matter at all."

I've had these conversations by the dozens. They become a great opportunity to talk about what a fulfilling life could look like. And if indeed there is an eternity where one gives an account of their life to the Creator, you will probably want to have a pretty good answer ready. It may or may not require a career change. It may be only a slight adjustment. It may simply be an articulation of why it is you do what you do and how you do it. But in any case, it's time to invest your life.

A pastor in Florida asked me to speak at his church: "I want you to speak on stewardship. We're trying to raise over half a million dollars that day to pay off our new family center."

I said, "No. I'm going to speak on discipleship."

"No, that won't work. I really want you to come, but I need you to speak on stewardship."

I said, "If you only speak on stewardship, then all you get is their check. Let me speak on discipleship and how to invest your life and one of the applications will be finances. I think we can pay off this building in a day, but don't just go after the money. Go after the heart and soul."

Very cautiously, he agreed.

I spoke from Mark 8, which is the famous story where Jesus feeds a multitude of people by miraculously multiplying a few loaves of bread. The chapter ends with the haunting words, "For what does it profit a man to gain the whole world, but forfeit his soul?"

Two clear outcomes came from that day: 1) they raised enough money for the new building and, 2) there were more than a dozen men and one woman, who came up to me and said, "You kind of ruined my life. I was really happy writing checks, but now you're telling me I also have to invest my life."

I was speaking at a men's mentoring group on the north side of Chicago about how to invest their lives and their money in the kingdom of God. To the talented young business executives I said, "Now that you have become a follower of Jesus, how are you going to fund the kingdom in a way that pays the biggest dividends?"

During our 30 hours together, it was fascinating to watch the mentoring that took place between the guys who had already begun to figure this out, and those who were very new to this. There were many conversations that would make God Himself smile and have leaders of organizations in ministry wondering,

"How do I get to be invited to one of these? I'd love to raise some money here."

One night, well after midnight, a young man wanted to have a conversation about how to best invest what he had been given. He held a law degree and an MBA, and was the head of an investment firm in the Twin Cities. His wife and he had picked out the house of their dreams, discovered it was owned by one of the Minnesota Twins and had their real-estate agent contact his sports agent to say, "If you ever move, we would like the right of first refusal on your house."

Within a year, the player was traded and this young couple negotiated a deal on the beautiful lake view house. This young man had everything he had ever dreamed of, but he was telling me that he felt like he wanted to leave his investment firm and go, "into ministry."

I listened to him for a while before interrupting him, saying, "I'm listening to you talk about your life, and it feels as though you're a sort of soul-shepherd for the people around the lake. You and your wife have held couples' groups, seminars, Bible studies and individual coaching sessions with many of them. Why don't you consider that ministry? Have you ever considered that most professional 'ministers' do not get the same opportunities that you guys get?"

He responded, "I never thought of it that way."

It has now been 15 years. We've stayed in close touch and this couple has invested their lives and resources well, both around the lake and in the larger kingdom of God.

You have been given a life that's uniquely yours. Invest it well, without pressure, without guilt, without shame, but rather with anticipation and forward-thinking.

QUESTIONS FOR FURTHER REFLECTION

1. What are the keys resources I have to invest?

2. Can I identify/list ways that I have actively negated the op-portunities I have been given?

ACTION PLAN

1. Identify areas of my life where I feel that I "get it." Create a plan of action for how to become aware or informed in areas where I "don't get it."

2. Dream big and consider ways my life could be more fulfilled if I took some risks and made the most of opportunities that may lie in front of me.

CHAPTER 6

IT'S TIME TO UPDATE
YOUR VIEW OF GOD

Through the course of this book, we've dealt with your dark side, your past and your greatest limitation. You've realized that it's time to invest the one life God has given you, but now, it's time to update your view of God.

For this chapter, we are going to return to Psalm 103. I know what you are thinking, 'One Psalm for two chapters? This guy must not know his Bible very well.' But here's the thing that has always amazed me about the scriptures. God creates the entire world, from black void to the Sabbath, in one chapter, but holy men and women like Joshua and Ruth, get their own books. This is because God can create a world with a swipe of His hand, but to find a truly willing spirit; now that's something special.

Psalm 103 is one of those special chapters for me which can be read over and over, always gleaning new dimensions of God: "Praise the Lord, O my soul, and forget not all his benefits, who forgives all your sins and heals all your diseases, who redeems your life from the pit and crowns you with love and compassion."

In this chapter, instead of using the passage to find freedom from your past, I want to use it to give you some portraits of your Father in Heaven.

If you were to go out into the streets, and ask people, 'what's God like?' you'd get some really wild answers.

There would be some who wouldn't have much to say at all.

Others would say that God is like a mythological character: big chest, broad shoulders, a beard, wielding some sort of massive weapon that He'll hit you with if you make one mistake or He's mad about something.

And still others would imagine God as this great cosmic sky-muffin that just wants the world to be one big group hug.

These may all be part of the story, but I want you consider the image of God as the Father who heals your soul, "who forgives all your sins and…crowns you with love and compassion."

One's personal view of God is often learned through our families. For many of you, that makes for a very misconstrued view of God. In the households you grew up in, how many of you were, 'crowned with love and compassion'?

I used to live and work in western Canada. We used to say, "Western Canadian men have two feelings: good and bad."

If you ask a western Canadian man, "Tell me what's going on, what are you feeling?"

He'd say, "I'm feeling bad."

"Can you be more specific?"

"Real bad?"

When I first went to Western Australia, I spoke at a men's conference. I mentioned this, and a bloke shouted, "Australian men have two feelings too, bad and not bad."

No one laughed.

I asked the rest of the men if he was right, and there was a wave of indecipherable, caveman-like grunts.

I've heard so many stories of people whose fathers were always in a bad mood, or in a not-bad mood; men who walked around the house sort of hunched over, grumbling and grunting.

That's not what your Father in Heaven is like. According to Psalm 103:

Verse 6, "He is on your side."

Verse 8, "He is compassionate and he is gracious...he is slow to anger...he abounds in love towards us."

Verse 9, "He does not accuse us."

Verse 10, "He does not treat us as we deserve."

That sounds like an amazing Father in heaven.

One Sunday morning, I spoke at Soul Survivor church in England. Afterwards, the pastor took me to lunch at a little street café in the shadow of Windsor Castle. As we finished he said, "So what are you speaking on tonight?"

I replied, "I didn't know I was. I didn't bring anything."

"You've read your Bible, you know what to do."

I had been reading Psalm 103, so I thought, 'That's a nice passage. It'll be brief, but meaningful. I like those.'

That night at church, more people showed up than ever before. They had to tear down the food tables in the back and move everything out. Soul Survivor church doesn't have pews, or even chairs. You just sit cross-legged on the floor or lie down and close your eyes, or lean against a friend or stranger. This night, they had people packed in everywhere. I just had a little clearing to stand in. No pulpit, no stool, nowhere to move.

I looked out over the audience and nearly everyone was under 30, many were under 20. There were all sorts of styles of hair and clothing. There were spikes and chains and bright colors contrasting lots of black.

I remember looking at them and thinking, 'I want these young people in 21st century London to get the picture of God the Psalmist was trying to paint over 2,000 years ago.'

So I simply said, "I have children about your age. Some of your parents' wish they could have done a better job, but they just couldn't. I want to say to you, as a father, I'm sorry. I'm sorry we weren't better parents to you. I wish we could have done better, but some of us just couldn't. I'm sorry for breaking our promises, for releasing our frustrations on you, for hurting you physically and emotionally, for failing to live up to the image of your Father in heaven. Will you forgive us and release us?"

They were all staring at me, and I thought, 'Well, let's go back to the text,' but people just sort of lost it.

It started as a murmur in the back, and slowly worked its way up to my little circle in the front. People had their arms around each other; they were crying or praying aloud.

I thought, 'I've gotta wrap this up quick.' So I said, "Here's what the rest of the evening looks like. We're gonna sing a song, and we're just going to pray for you."

Matt Redman was the worship leader, and I said, "Matt, please sing something for us." He stood up and said, "I wrote a song this week." He started singing, "Heart of Worship."

That night, hundreds of young Londoners hugged, cried, and sought out adults who were old enough to be their parents, for affirmation and blessing.

We hold on to so much junk and baggage, but God doesn't want you to carry that stuff around with you. He wants to release you. The amazing God of the universe, the Father of your soul, offers you Himself. He forgives you. He heals you. He redeems you. He crowns you with love and compassion. He simply wants to be your Father and He wants you to represent him well in your own families.

QUESTIONS FOR FURTHER CONSIDERATION

1. When I consider the benefits of God (healing, restoring, forgiving, renewing), is there one I need or want to take greater advantage of?

2. Are there any images of God that it's time to let go of?

ACTION PLAN

1. Meditate on Psalm 103, updating my view of God.

2. Make a list of the things that I enjoy or appreciate about God. For example: He's always there. He listens. He cares. He forgives. Now write down three ways I can demonstrate that to my children.

   a.

   b.

   c.

IT'S TIME TO LOVE GOD WITH ALL YOUR HEART

Some of your Bibles have chapter headings. I'm always fascinated that it was someone's job to create those. The most common heading for Luke chapter 7, beginning in verse 36, is: "Jesus is Anointed by a Sinful Woman." Wouldn't you like to be her? 2000 years later and she's simply known as, "The Sinful Woman." That's a hard one to live down. Even if you say, "I changed. Do you still have to call me the Sinful Woman?" Most people, unfortunately, aren't as forgiving as Jesus.

Verse 36 says: "One of the Pharisees invited Jesus to have dinner with him and so He went to the Pharisee's house and re-clined at the table." In the Middle East, tables are about two feet high. You have pillows and can lean back; it's great for eating. Hard on the back, but otherwise it works quite well.

So Jesus and Simon (probably a bunch of other people as well) were having dinner at a respected religious leader's home, and in bursts a women that had 'led a sinful life' and she throws herself on the ground, weeping and using her tears and hair to clean Jesus' feet, then bathes them in perfume.

I don't care what era or part of the world you're from, this is just strange. We have here a males only dinner party and in burst a woman who has a reputation for not being the godliest of women, crashing the party with a bizarre mix of weeping and extreme PDA.

Now, a woman crying probably makes men more uncomfortable than anything else in the world. And men know that; we just don't know what to do about it, because for the most part, they're smarter than us.

So, the Sinful Woman begins weeping, cleaning and kissing Jesus' feet. What I find interesting about this is that Jesus doesn't make a big deal about it; He goes on as if it was a fairly normal occurrence in his life.

In verse 40, Simon asked, "Does He not know what kind of woman this is?"

Jesus said, "Simon, I have something to tell you."

"Tell me."

"Two men owed money to a certain moneylender, one of them five hundred denarii, the other only fifty. Neither one of them had the money to pay him back, so he cancelled the debts of both. Now, which one of them loves him more?"

Simon replied, "I suppose the one with the bigger debt."

"You have answered correctly."

This is one of those classic Jesus stories for two reasons.

One, He always sides with those who are forgotten, over-looked, and scorned. Jesus honors them as people. I love that about Him.

But it's also a classic Jesus story because He asks, "Which one loves more?" That is the key question in this passage.

Jesus then turned towards the woman, saying, "Simon, do you see this woman?"

I'm sure Simon's thinking, "See her? How can I miss her?"

Jesus said, "You gave me no water for my feet when I came in."

This would have been standard practice in the Middle East back then. It was dry, dusty, and they wore sandals; they washed their feet a lot.

Jesus then said, "You didn't give me any water, but she's wet my feet with her tears and wiped them with her hair. Simon, you didn't even give me a kiss."

Even now in the Middle East, when men greet other men, they kiss on the cheek. Depending on the relationship between the two men, it's either both cheeks or back and forth three times; once, I even saw four. I don't get it, but they seem to have it figured out and rarely have that awkward moment when one person pulls back too early and leaves the other kissing thin air.

Jesus continued, "But you see, this woman, from the time I entered, has not stopped kissing my feet. Simon, you didn't even put oil on my head, yet she has poured perfume on my feet. Therefore, I tell you, her many sins have been forgiven, for she has loved much."

The two things we need to talk about as this passage unfolds are forgiveness and love.

Let's start with forgiveness.

In the 21st century, the best word for forgiveness is probably, 'release'. Many Christians are cognitively aware that they believe in forgiveness, but they don't necessarily feel forgiven. Jesus wants to bridge that gap.

The story of the Sinful Woman is interesting because she was one of…you know, 'those kind of girls'. But then she became one of 'them'. You know those annoying people who are just so darn happy about their new life in Christ. They jump up and down and sing real loud and hug and pray for everyone. And although that's one form of *expressing* the joy of being forgiven, it's only one possible response, it's not the essence of being free. Freedom is a state of being. It's an experience. The ironic part is, you don't need to actually do anything with your freedom. In fact, its primary function is how you feel within yourself.

I spoke briefly about an assessment tool that helps you identify your greatest strength. Another one we often use in helping people identify the best of who they are is called the 16PF (16 Personality Factors, created by Raymond Cattell and his team). This tool doesn't assess your preferences, but rather your inherent personality. When I took it, it showed that I lacked compassion and had a tendency towards anger.

As soon as I got home I showed my report to Dianna and said, "I want you to read this. Just tell me, am I really this bad?"

She read it and said, "Martin, I remember when you were like this." Then there was a long silence, and she said, "I remember when you came to Christ, how much you changed. If ever you don't walk with him, this is what you'll be like again. It's not very nice."

See, I had been forgiven of my sins when I came to Christ, and it changed me. Not only my behavior, but how I felt, so I forgot that I had some pretty bad tendencies.

Like me, Simon thought he was the good guy. But the problem with that is, you can become self-righteous and develop a religious spirit.

A religious spirit is when you substitute religious activity for the presence and power of the Holy Spirit. The religious spirit calculates. It keeps track. You want credit for how many good things you've done, how often you read your Bible, how many times you show up at church. You evaluate yourself and others by quantifiable benchmarks. This tendency often creeps into really good people and it limits their ability to forgive, and to love. What's dangerous about the religious spirit is that it's easy to forget that the grace of God is available for other people too. Simon forgot that the grace of God is about love, and love is the greatest of all the commandments: Love the Lord your God with all you heart, and soul, and mind, and strength.

I was speaking at a conference a couple years ago, and a guy came up to me and said, "Martin, I hold a campfire at night. I'd like you to come."

I said, "I'm tied up 'til 11."

"We'll be there past midnight."

I showed up at 11:10. The women had all gone to bed and there were twelve men sitting around the fire. I came in through the darkness and sat down. It was not very stimulating; I understood why the women had gone to bed. I was there close to 10 minutes and thought, 'I'm not staying much longer.' Just then, someone says, "We don't get someone like Martin here very often."

When someone says that, you think, 'What's that supposed to mean?' But the man explained, "Martin, here's what we want. You always talk about going to the next level. Give us the secret of going to the next level with God."

I looked around and thought to myself, 'I didn't know there was a secret. Nobody told me the secret.' I thought, 'Do I give them what they want, or do I give them what they need?'

So I said, "Guys, I need to know my audience. I have one question. Do you love God with all your heart? No discussion, no qualifiers. It's a simple 'yes' or 'no'."

All but one answered with a resounding, "No."

So I stood up and said, "Here's the deal, I'll be back tomorrow night at 11 o'clock. You do whatever it takes. You fast, you pray, you go back to the Old Testament, you pluck your beard, hair, rip your clothes. There's some sand over there by the beach, go stick your face in it 'til you can't breathe and then stay a little longer. You do whatever it takes, so that when the question is asked again, it's a 'Yes'."

I got up and walked away, assuming that I didn't earn any friends that night. I was walking through the darkness, when I heard footsteps behind me. I turned around and one of the guys said, "Do you know who was back there?"

I answered, "No, only the guy who invited me."

He says, "There's two, maybe three of us that are worth well over $50 million, a couple maybe over a hundred. One guy's over a hundred and fifty."

"What's your point?" I asked.

He said, "Those guys could've funded your entire ministry."

I said, "Do I look like the kind of guy who'd sell my soul for a few million? You don't get to come back tomorrow night. You need two days to fast and pray. Seriously, don't come back for two days."

The next night I showed up at 11 o'clock, and there were eleven men sitting around the fire.

I said, "No discussion, you know the plan. Do you love God with all your heart?"

All eleven gave a resounding, "Yes."

I said, "Okay, now we can have the real conversation."

Our conversation lasted 'til 2:30 am in the morning. It was the kind of conversation most men never get to have. It was unguarded and honest. It was about connecting deeply with God, and your family. We talked about how to be a man of passion, not just a man of function.

By lunch the next day, seven of the eleven men's wives found me. I'd never met any of them, but they hugged, kissed and thanked me, saying, "I don't know what the conversation was about –he won't tell me, but my husband seems different."

The men around the fire were good guys. They took care of their families and gave money and time to their churches and communities. But they forgot, just as Simon had, that it's all about love.

Simon had a religious spirit that crept into his life and defined the way he saw himself and others. The Sinful Woman went from bondage to freedom through her reckless love and devotion to Jesus.

Whether you're a sinful woman, a business executive, or just some average person, the question is, "Do you love God with all your heart, mind, soul and body? Because here's the hard truth, you're not going to see real, sustainable, authentic life change by half-assing it.

It's either 'Yes', or 'No'.

QUESTIONS FOR FURTHER REFLECTION

1. Can I identify any ways I have adopted the religious spirit?

2. Are there any limitations I have placed on my expressions of faith or love for God?

ACTION PLAN

1. Pray, "Lord, can I be one of those people who love You with
    all of my heart?"

2. Write down three ways I will express that this week, and
    then do them!

    a.

    b.

    c.

CHAPTER 8

IT'S TIME TO TAKE A FRESH LOOK AT THE FUTURE

I love to see God's dreams for people and the way folks light up when they talk about what they feel God has in store for them.

When I was a young minister, I came up with this brilliant idea that God is looking for people that He can bless and use. I began spending more and more time thinking and praying about what type of person God uses, I found that there were little to no patterns. No clear indicators to say, 'Now this is the type of person God uses.'

Tom, one of the guys that I've mentored over the years is one of those unlikely candidates. If you spend time with him, he'll seem kind of, lackluster. Yet everywhere Tom goes, the hand of God just seems to rest upon him. Recently he's led a small Canadian church to a thriving congregation of 3,500 people. One example of the effect he has on those around him is that the city gave their church a million-dollar grant to build a skateboard park because the church was doing a better job with the youth than the local government agencies. Younger ministers and church leaders flock to Tom, asking, "How do I become one of those people that God can bless and use?"

Tom usually answers, "Honestly, you probably don't want to be focused enough to go to the next level."

Joshua and Caleb were the type of people that God could use.

Joshua chapter 14, starting at verse 6, reads: "Caleb said to Joshua, 'I was forty years old when Moses, the servant of the Lord sent me to explore the land. I brought back a report according to what was in my heart, according to my convictions.'"

Whenever you're taking a good look at your future, it's useful to remember your original dreams. Now, we already discussed that almost no one gets the life they dreamed of. When you're dreaming your dreams for life, you never count on disappointments or setbacks. No one ever counts on health issues or personal loss or financial recessions. Yet, when we look back and see these setbacks, we can still look forward with renewed idealism.

One of the fascinating things about Joshua and Caleb is that in the midst of all the difficulties they faced, they never lost sight of the original ideal. They would always say, "God has promised this land to us. It's ours."

Some of you probably know friends who are always upbeat. The future's always looking so grand that they don't deal with what is actually in front of them. Optimism is good, but it's also necessary for us to take an honest look at who we are and what kind of lives we want to live. The difficult part is getting from where we presently are, to where we dream God is taking us, all while facing the difficulties life consistently presents. This is where faith comes in.

In Joshua 14, Caleb and eleven other men went to spy out the land. They all saw the same thing, but Caleb saw things very differently than the others. Caleb says, "My brothers who went up with me, made the hearts of the [Israelites] melt with fear; but I followed the Lord my God fully."

Where you view God in your life makes a big difference in how you see both your past and future. Active faith in God can allow you to look back and say, "I used to have this dream. What happened? Maybe I gave up too easily? Maybe God wasn't done yet."

That's the difference between dreamers, fantasizers and visionaries.

Dreamers have a vague idea of where they want to go, but they don't have any clear plans or strategies on how to get there.

Then there's the fantasizer. The fantasizer spends huge amounts of time and energy, thinking and talking about the dream, but with limited follow-through.

Finally, there's the true visionary. Visionaries have the same dream, but they also have the discipline, courage, and faith to see their dreams become realities.

In Joshua 14, when Moses heard Caleb's optimistic report, he said, "The land on which your feet have walked will be your inheritance and that of your children forever, because you have followed the Lord my God wholeheartedly."

Now, if someone in church stood up and said, "I followed the Lord wholeheartedly all my days," most of us would probably pray for humility for that person. But Caleb made a clear choice not to be one of those people who got distracted and side-tracked by all the criticism. He chose to keep his eyes clearly focused on God. God honors people with that kind of faith.

When I first started as a professor, it was at the Canadian Theological Seminary in Regina, Saskatchewan. There, in the dead of winter, skin can freeze in three seconds. The good part is people tend to spend a lot of time together indoors, talking. I was very young for a professor, so the graduate students tended to come by my office and talk. As these young men spoke, it became clear to me that their ideals of the type of men they wanted to be, often didn't match their public persona or their private lives. And I'm not just talking about blatant sin. They said they wanted to be men of God, but they were arrogant, judgmental and cutting to others.

Caleb had what we call "a congruent life." His public and private persona matched. His dreams were in line with God's plans for him. His actions were in line with this faith.

Have you ever been around someone, who makes everyone feel good, cared for and generally warm? They just have a spirit that makes you feel different, special, better.

Caleb was one of those kinds of people. He had a distinct character. He had a 'different kind of spirit.' He had a focus and purpose that allowed him to override distractions, obstacles and setbacks. He didn't succumb to the negativity during the children of Israel's forty years in the wilderness.

We live in a complaining culture. The children of Israel lived in one as well, but for Caleb, the different kind of spirit, did not allow circumstances to dictate the outcomes. Forty years in the wilderness could get a little old, but for Caleb, it was just part of the journey of faith; part of the necessary steps to achieving God's dreams and plans for him and his people.

As the passage wraps up in verses 10 to 12, it's time to realize the dream.

Caleb says, "Just as the Lord has promised, he's kept me alive for the forty-five years since we moved about in the desert. Here I am today, eighty-five years old! And I am as strong today as the day Moses sent me out."

Looking at Caleb's story, we can conclude that there are three main limitations to fulfilling God's dreams for our lives.

1) Too much is about you, and not enough is about God.
    This happens to good people. This happens to good

churches. The key is to recognize this and bring God into focus.

2) We lose heart because the promises that God made take too long to materialize, so we just give up.

3) We place limited focus on character and integrity. We keep focusing on what we're going to do, instead of who we're going to be.

When dreaming with God about our futures, we also have to keep in mind, that anytime we make changes, we have to ask, 'what do I leave behind, and what do I embrace? What do I change and what do I fix? What are the greatest limitations and resources that I possess? What do I have to do to maintain an authentic faith? What do I have to do to see my dreams become reality?'

QUESTIONS FOR FURTHER REFLECTION

1. Can I identify three ways that I have placed limitations on God for my future?

2. The last time I was faced with a significant challenge, was God in focus, or somewhere in the periphery?

3. Can I go back and identify any unfulfilled promises that I feel God made to me?

ACTION PLAN

1. Ask God to complete those unfulfilled promises.

2. Go back to faded dreams for my life, and ask God to re-
    awaken them.

CHAPTER 9

IT'S NOW TIME

I think of life change in three parts:

1) Starting Change. This consists of small steps, one-by-
   one. The bulk of life change consists of simply putting
   one foot in front of the other.

2) Long-term change. This consists of significant milestones. There's usually only a handful of those in the
   course of your life.

3) Profound change. These are the changes in your behavior, paradigm and soul that alter the way you view and
   relate to yourself, others, and God. These are the kinds
   of changes God is most interested in because they af-
   fect not only yourself, but all those who you interact
   with, sending a ripple effect through your family, your
   church, your community, and the world.

To demonstrate this, I want to look at two case studies of life change, both occurring in Africa.

A few years ago, I was leading a team to Nigeria. We were conducting a series of conferences with church and community leaders. With us we had students, master speakers, a doctor and a dentist. It was a good time, and God was with us.

Thousands of pastors showed up for our two-day conferences, but we also spent time in orphanages and prisons, attempting to represent Christ in small ways on a one-on-one basis. The first lady of Nigeria heard about our work, and invited us to the state house to make a presentation.

We assumed our meeting would be something informal, small, and short, a sort of quaint formality, like the African equivalent to high tea with the queen. When we entered however, the press was there, their cameras rolling. We sat at a large conference table with the first lady and other government officials and discussed our work in the country.

We made the evening news and front page of the national newspaper. We had organized a Business and Government Outreach for the following Saturday, and because of the publicity, it became national fanfare. We had to switch venues to the largest banquet hall we could find, yet hundreds more showed up than there were seats available. The room was abuzz with energy as people ate and chatted.

I remember standing off to the side, looking out across the room and thinking, "This is exciting and all, but I have to remember, that God is doing something here. This is not about me. He has a message and simply wants to use me to deliver it to a room full of his potential servants."

Africa is a wonderful and amazing continent full of the best and worst of what our world has to offer. Even the land is full of extremes, from snowcapped mountains to great rifts and valleys, from jungle rainforest to barren dessert. Its people are full of so much love, joy and music, yet are also capable of some of the worst examples of violence and horror the world has ever seen.

What was interesting to me is that in such a varied continent, with all sorts of wonders and problems, the thing everyone focused on when talking about change, was corruption. Whether it was in business, government or the church, corruption seemed to be at the very core of the troubles.

My book, *The Power of Mentoring,* had just been printed in West Africa, and we passed out free copies to everyone in the room. I was surprised by how many people had already read, and wanted to discuss it. It seemed the book's character-based leadership model resonated in that cultural context.

Of all the moments, conversations and results to come out of that night and our time in Nigeria, the conversation that has stuck with me most was with a very intelligent physician, a man of wisdom and a pillar of his community.

He told me, "Africa has brought in teachers, politicians, religious leaders and businessmen, to help us change and fix our many problems. But all their models attempted to impart their own ways of doing things. Your character-based model, changes from the inside out. That's the kind of change we have to have if we're going see the impact in Africa we want and need."

He went on, "When I came to do medical training in the U.S., I was surprised by how much attention, resources and study were spent on addictions. It seemed to be everywhere, just under the surface. In America, it seems to me, everyone thinks someone else has a worse addiction than themselves, yet everyone has some sort of addiction, whether it's heroin, alcohol, food, sex, nicotine or caffeine. But they can always point to someone else and say, 'Yes, but I'm not as bad as them'. It's the same with corruption in Africa. Everyone's part of it, but there's always someone worse. In America, there is a lot of emphasis on changing the behavior, but not the character of the addict. So, if we want to change Africa, we cannot just address corruption, we have to change, from the inside-out."

The second case study I want to give you takes us two thousand miles northeast, to Egypt, when the children of Israel were fighting for their freedom.

At the end of Exodus chapter 7, there's just been a plague that turned the Nile River into blood. Besides being disgusting, it was poisonous to plants, animals and people. The Nile was the lifeline of Egypt. It wasn't like here and now, where we simply turn on the faucet and clean, safe water comes pouring out. Back then, if the river flowed with blood, everything died. Then after seven days with no water, here comes the frogs.

Exodus chapter 8 reads: "The LORD says: Let my people go, so that they might worship me. If you refuse to let them go, I will plague your whole country with frogs."

When you are attempting to implement authentic life change, it's important to assess your resources. Frogs did not seem a likely resource for assailing the king of the greatest empire in the world, but that's what God decided to use.

I want to look at this situation from Pharaoh's side. Pharaoh's in charge, always has been, always will be. That's just the way it is. Nobody ever stood up to him. It was probably the first time anybody had ever said, "You had better, or else."

Furthermore, the person finally saying, "You had better or else," was a slave leader, saying, "You better let all the slaves do what they want, or I'm going to, um, send...um, frogs."

Often, the things that make us realize something has to change aren't grand milestones or catastrophes, but little annoying things that just won't go away.

2006 was an interesting year for me. Dianna and I spent the first two weeks of the year in Florida. It was a mid-winter getaway: a bit of writing, a lot of relaxing and getting ready for the year to come.

I remember saying to her, "I wish I could skip '06. In '07 I have the sort of schedule I'm looking for, but there's too much in '06 and I can't cancel any of it. It's busier than I want it to be, but I promise I'm changing. '07, '08, '09, that's how my life is gonna be. I just gotta get through '06."

I flew back to New York on Monday night to teach the following day and while I was eating lunch on Tuesday, I had a heart attack. In the hospital they asked, "Have you been under a lot of stress?"

When I realized that I had a heart attack after a two-week vacation, I knew it was time to change. I knew it, my family knew it, God knew it. In my mind, I had a year. But when it was time to change, it was time to change and there was no way around it. Sadly enough, I didn't change before it was too late. The ironic part is that when I was on the beach in early January, I thought it was too late to change the upcoming year, but after a heart attack, that year changed very quickly.

When you find yourself in a place where you know it's time to change, but you look at the circumstances and say, "I can't, it's impossible," the odds are it isn't, and that is probably the time when changes are needed most.

Let's pick up the story again in verse 3: Moses says to Pharaoh, "The Nile will teem with frogs. They'll come up into your palace, into your bedroom, under your bed, the houses of your officials, on your people, into your ovens, your kneading troughs."

Moses wanted to give very specific details. We're not just talking frogs. We're talking lots of frogs, everywhere, in everything. He wanted to make sure Pharaoh understood, it may just be frogs, but this was going to be big.

When attempting to make life changes, it's important to consider all of your available resources, whether that's frogs or the awesome power of God. Then, one of your jobs is to figure out which part God is responsible for, and which part you are responsible for.

In 2006, I was responsible for taking care of my health. My job was to create a schedule and a healthy life pattern that ensured I was able to continue doing God's work. I didn't do my part, and so God couldn't do His part through me. I wasn't able to keep doing what I'd been doing for fifty years, but so often, it's just too easy to do the same old thing.

Take the Pharaoh. He thought the Israelites would always be his slaves, but then the Nile turned to blood and those darn frogs showed up. When the status quo changed, Pharaoh stubbornly stuck to what he'd always known, and he summoned his own holy men: "And the magicians did the same with their secret arts, making frogs come up on the land of Egypt."

When I read this I think, 'Wait. Timeout. They already had frogs everywhere, and now they want double frogs?'

But so often, we just keep on doing the same thing, even when it's not working. Two weeks before I had my heart attack, I knew I was stressed, knew I was tired. I knew I worked too hard in '05, and now I was about to work too hard in '06. I had a chance to stop it, but instead I said, "Here's an idea, how about I double a bad thing. Instead of having one stressful year, how about I have two."

I think the secret arts magicians got an earful from the boss, because after the whole double-frog debacle, Pharaoh summoned Moses and Aaron, and said, "You pray to the Lord that these frogs will get away from me and my people, and then I'll let your people go and sacrifice to the Lord."

When you're reading a passage like this, it's hard to tell the tone of the conversation. Is Pharaoh very humbly saying, "Um, can I ask that you please make these frogs go away?"

Or is this a command? "You, get these frogs outta here! Do whatever it takes, I just want them gone!"

What we do know, is that when the frogs doubled, Pharaoh knew he needed a change, but he still wasn't willing to make the necessary sacrifices. He was still blaming other people and looking for a magic solution to his problem.

I love Moses' response here. He says, "I leave with you the honor of setting the time for me to pray for you and your officials and your people, that your houses may be rid of the frogs except for those that will remain in the Nile."

One of the ways God honors us, is that He doesn't impose his will. He doesn't come along and say, "It's time and you know it."

You see, the great God of the universe, the Father of your soul, the One who is most interested in your life, is saying, "I can help you change, but you need to decide when you're ready."

He sets before you the honor of setting your own timeline. He doesn't force it. He doesn't make you. Sometimes it feels like that'd be easier, but if He did that, our will would be violated. Even if our behavior is endangering ourselves, our health or our loved ones, He still won't override our will.

Pharaoh's response in verse 10 is unbelievable. He says, "Mmm, tomorrow."

Tomorrow! Pharaoh, timeout! You could fix this frog thing right here, right now, but you want to wait until tomorrow!

But that's a common response. Diets start tomorrow. People quit smoking tomorrow. People change everything, tomorrow, next week, next year. It's almost never today. But today is the day of life change. Tomorrow is the day of excuses.

We know it's time for a change. We determine what it is, what needs to happen and establish a timeline for the change, but then we have to find the will, courage and discipline to actually see it through.

As we wrap up this passage, we find one of the clearest principles of life change found anywhere in recorded history, at least from my humble perspective.

Verse 13: "The Lord did what Moses asked. The frogs died in the houses, in the courtyards, in the fields. They were piled high into great heaps and the whole land reeked of them."

Finally in verse 15: "But when Pharaoh saw that there was relief, he hardened his heart."

Very often we just want relief; we don't really want life change. We want the symptoms to just go away. We don't want to actually fix the problem. We'll promise most anything for relief, but when it becomes our responsibility to actually deliver on our part, we renege.

Now I want you to pause, and get into your favorite reflective posture. As you look at your next stage of life change, form a clear picture in your mind. You want to make it real. It's not simply a hope, a dream or a fantasy. As the picture becomes clear, begin to look around. Where is God? How big is He? Who else is in the picture? Now close your eyes and take however long necessary to complete this process.

Life change approaches range from, identifying and developing productive next steps to going after your dark side, and whether you identify with the Rich Young Ruler or the Sinful Woman, whether you see yourself more like Pharaoh with the frogs or the young leaders in Germany, life change always asks these two simple questions:

What do I leave behind?

What do I embrace and ask the Father for?

The Great God Almighty, creator of the world and Father of your soul, loves you dearly. He wants the best for you. He dreams big things for you. He wants you to be at peace, both

with yourself and with others. He wants you to love both yourself and Him. He wants you to have a great life. But in order
to do that, you must partner with your Father in heaven, deal
with your dark side, make peace with your past, take stock of
your resources and get to a place where you love God with all of
your heart. He's worth it. You're worth it. It's time. It's time for
a change.

QUESTIONS FOR FURTHER REFLECTION

1. What excuses do I use that keep me from receiving the best
    of what God has for me?

2. What area of my life do I need to experience renewed life
    change?

ACTION PLAN

1. Identify two reasons why I haven't changed more?

2. Identify two things I'm going to leave behind and two
    things I'm going to embrace that will help take me to the
    "next level."

    To Leave Behind:

    a.

    b.

    To Embrace:

    a.

    b.

SUGGESTED READING

Amen, D. (2000). *Change your brain, change your life: the breakthrough program for conquering anxiety, depression, obsessiveness, anger, and impulsiveness.* New York: Times Books.

Buckingham, M. (2007). *Go put your strengths to work: 6 powerful steps to achieve outstanding performance.* New York: Free Press.

Cloud, H. & Townsend, J. (2001). *How people grow: what the Bible reveals about personal growth.* Grand Rapids, Mich: Zondervan.

Lane, T. & Tripp, P. (2006). *How people change.* Winston-Salem, NC: Punch Press.

Norcross, J., Loberg, K. & Norcross, J. (2012). *Changeology: 5 steps to realizing your goals and resolutions.* New York: Simon & Schuster.

Patterson, K. (2008). *Influencer: the power to change anything.* New York: McGraw-Hill.

Quinn, R. (1996). *Deep change: discovering the leader within.* San Francisco, Calif: Jossey-Bass Publishers.

Rath, T. & Clifton, D. (2004). *How full is your bucket?: positive strategies for work and life.* New York: Gallup Press.

Rath, T. (2007). *Strengths finder 2.0.* New York: Gallup Press.

Trent, J. (2006). *The 2 degree difference: how small things can change everything.* Nashville, Tenn: Broadman & Holman Publishers.

Verghese, C. (2007). *Brain power: how to fine-tune your brain naturally.* Enumclaw, WA: WinePress Pub.

ABOUT THE AUTHOR

D r. Martin Sanders is president and founder of Global Leadership, Inc. and director of the Doctor of Ministry program at Alliance Theological Seminary (Nyack, NY). Dr. Sanders has taught at Canadian Theological Seminary (Regina, Saskatchewan) and at ATS for more than 25 years.

Dr. Sanders has crossed cultural, socio-economic, and gender lines in over thirty countries to make a lifestyle out of developing and mentoring people. He has the vision, passion, and skill to see development in leaders at both the local and global levels. Dr. Sanders has written a number of books, including *The Power of Mentoring: Shaping People Will Shape the World,* and is a highly sought after speaker around the world.

ABOUT GLOBAL LEADERSHIP, INC.

Global Leadership, Inc. is a non-profit organization focused on developing and empowering the next generation of effective Christian leaders, especially in under-resourced parts of the world. Since 1995, Global Leadership has been helping individuals and organizations by intentionally focusing on character formation and using highly personalized leadership development models.

"Global Leadership recognizes that raising leaders is a complex task. Before delving into the specifics of a particular developmental process, Global Leadership emphasizes the development of one's heart and soul. Global Leadership understands how crucial character is to leadership and pushes our leaders beyond their impressive skills to demonstrate lives of integrity."

Dr. Carson Pue

Executive Director, First Baptist Church, Vancouver, Canada

Former President, Arrow Leadership Ministries

Website

www.globalleadershipinc.org

Mail

Global Leadership

P.O. Box 527

Nyack, NY 10960

Phone

845.770.5751

ADDITIONAL GLOBAL LEADERSHIP RESOURCES

It's Time for a Change and all other resources are available for order on the Global Leadership website. (www.globalleadershipinc.org)

Overcoming the Roadblocks to Life Change DVD

The road towards life change is never easy or simple. It is filled with twists, turns and most discouraging of all, roadblocks. These hurdles can be in the form of unprocessed trauma, emotional blind spots, and faulty perspectives. Dr. Martin Sanders gives three essential rules that can help us overcome the blocks that have halted our journey and experience the miracle of life change.

The Power of Mentoring: Shaping People Who Will Shape the World

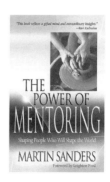

Mentoring is the indispensable tool in the spiritual and character formation of today's emerging leaders. As a coach, spiritual guide, parent, counselor and trusted friend, the mentor is someone who can pass his or her wisdom on to the next generation. With biblical examples of mentors and insights from experts in discipleship and mentor training, *The Power of Mentoring* provides practical strategies, exercises and models for your journey through mentoring. Discover why leaders around the world are using Dr. Martin Sanders' book to mentor the next generation of leaders.

How to Get the Family You've Always Wanted: Developing Healthy, Purposeful Families

Do you dream about having a great family? This book will give you the tools to have the family you've always wanted. Dr. Martin Sanders assists families with the balancing act of day-to-day living by offering realistic approaches, workable solutions and achievable outcomes.